T0055788

Musical PLANETS

8 ORIGINAL PIECES BY CAROLYN MILLER

ISBN 978-1-4803-5056-4

WILLIS MUSIC

EXCLUSIVELY DISTRIBUTED BY

HAL•LEONARD®
CORPORATION
7777 W. BLUEMOUND RD. P.O. BOX 13819 MILWAUKEE, WI 53213

Visit Hal Leonard Online at
www.halleonard.com

PERFORMANCE NOTES

By Carolyn Miller and Charmaine Siagian

MERCURY BLUES

Mercury, the smallest planet in our solar system, has an appearance similar to the moon: both are filled with craters. Mercury is also the planet closest to the sun—the blistering heat would certainly give anyone a severe case of the blues! This piece introduces the blues scale in the right hand beginning in measure 9, with the left hand playing the standard 12-bar blues chord progression.

VIVID VENUS

Venus—the brightest, most vivid planet—was named after the Roman goddess of love. This piece is really easier than it looks: don't let the key signature scare you. Before starting, familiarize yourself with both the G♭ pentascale as well as its whole-tone scale: G♭, A♭, B♭, C, D, E. As you play, see if you can effectively transmit gentleness and love via the "shooting stars."

FROM EARTH TO THE MOON

I was reminiscing about the countdown to the Apollo 11 rocket lift-off in 1969. The United States was about to send the first man to the moon, so there was lots of energy and excitement. All of the controls had to be tested, and there were frustrating delays leading up to the launch. (Find the "false start"!) In this piece, the rocket takes off in measure 56, sailing grandly into space at measure 62. As you practice, find specific patterns to help you memorize quicker, and be sure that you have a good rhythmic pulse for 6/8.

EXPLORING MARS

Scientists have long been conducting experiments on neighboring Mars. Even though humans have not yet set foot on the "Red Planet," let's pretend that day has finally arrived. Our fearless exploration of Mars begins excitedly and with some unusual spacey sounds; in particular, a tone cluster made up of three black keys. At measure 17 we are in strange surroundings, so the mood is different. What do you think happens in the last four measures? Should we turn and run back to the spaceship, or continue exploring?

JUMPIN' JUPITER

Jupiter is the largest planet in our solar system and has a rapid rotation. The staccato notes in this piece create lots of energy, so make them crisp. Learning the patterns will help you memorize and play with confidence. I love playing the finale run starting at measure 56: use firm fingers and make it sparkle!

THE ICY RINGS OF SATURN

As you play, you should feel as if you are floating in space, like the icy rings encircling Saturn. I would recommend that you learn the C whole-tone scale: C, D, E, F♯, G♯, A♯. Is it similar to the one in "Vivid Venus"? After you memorize the piece, use your imagination and experiment with a variety of dynamics.

URANUS SPINNING

Did you know that the planet Uranus spins on its side? The triplets should create a whirly, spinning feel, but keep them steady. A practice suggestion would be to play block chords in both hands from measures 13-16. In measure 24, put the pedal down after you play the first note. Aim for a dramatic ending: strong, clean triplets and big forte chords.

THE WINDS OF NEPTUNE

Planet Neptune was named after the Roman god of the sea. It is also known as an extremely windy planet, with recorded winds of over 1000 miles per hour. The 16th notes can represent swirly gusts or turbulent waves, but I also imagined peaceful lulls in measures 9-22, and at the very end.

CONTENTS

Mercury Blues

Carolyn Miller

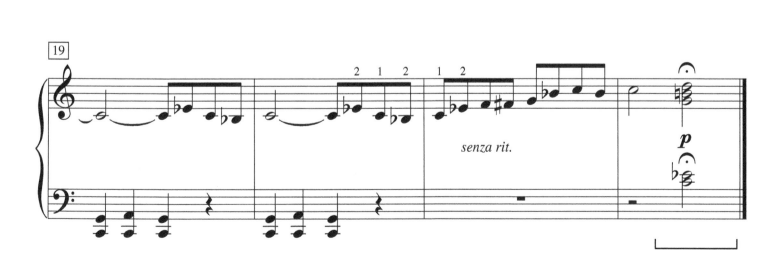

Vivid Venus

Carolyn Miller

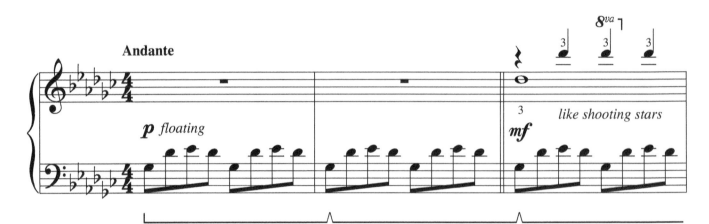

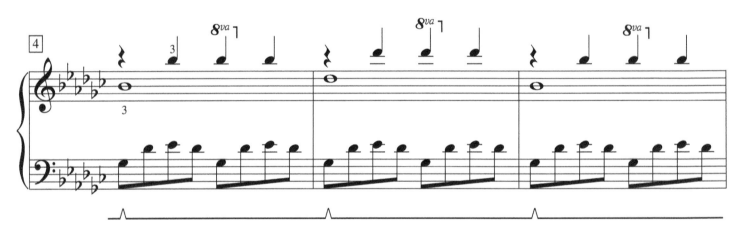

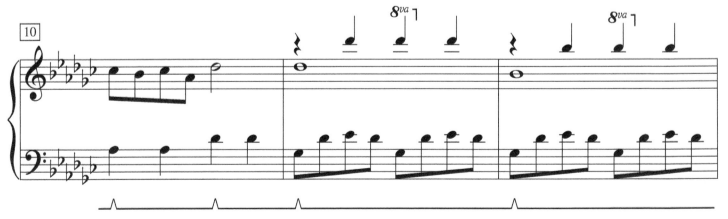

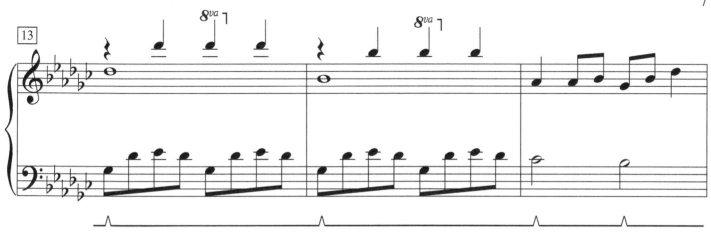

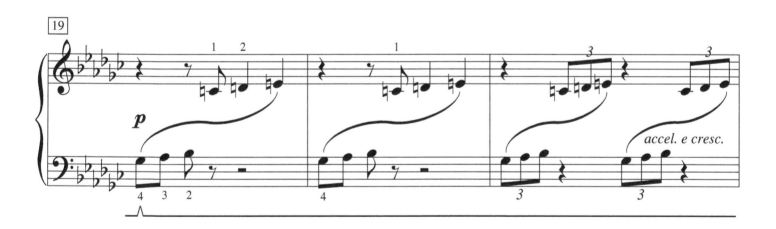

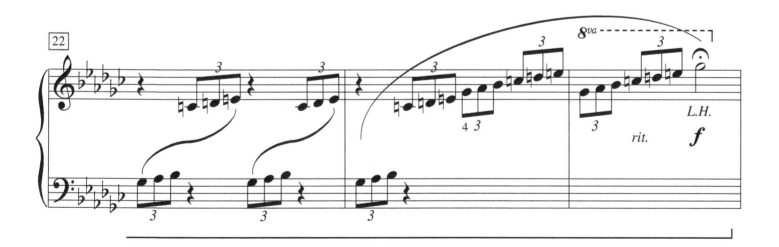

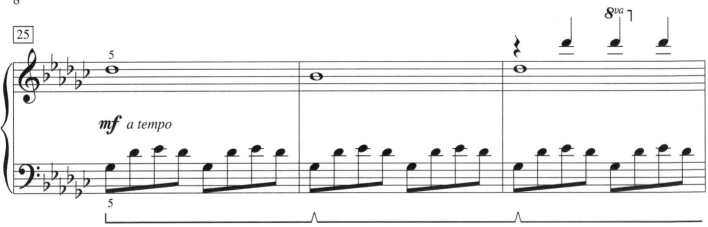

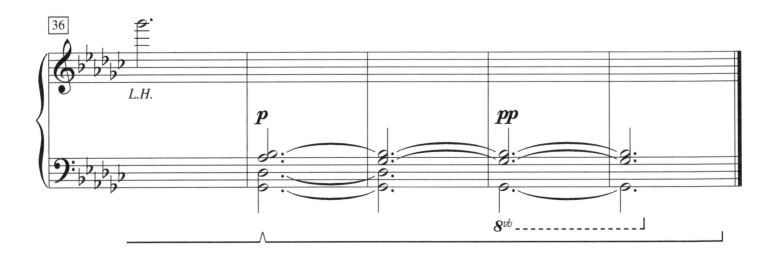

From Earth to the Moon

Carolyn Miller

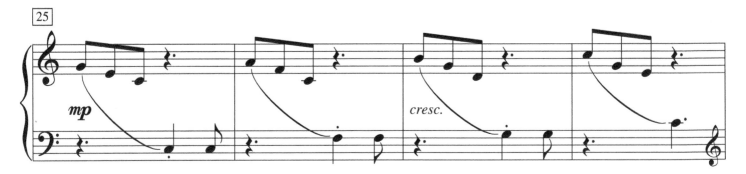

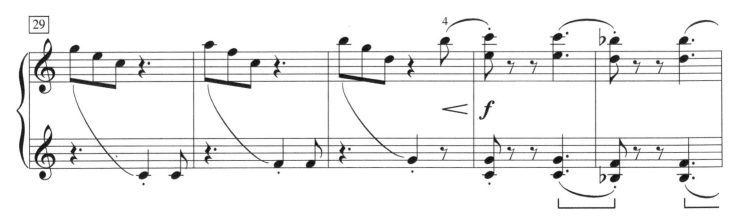

Exploring Mars

Carolyn Miller

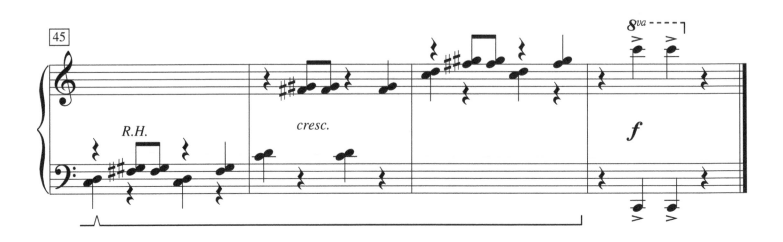

Jumpin' Jupiter

Carolyn Miller

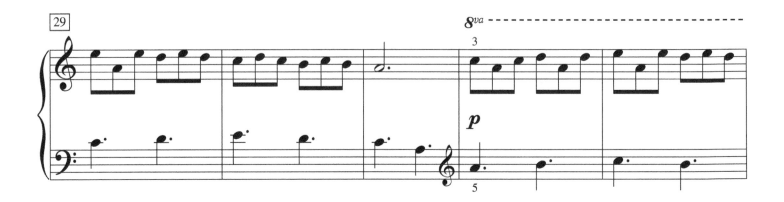

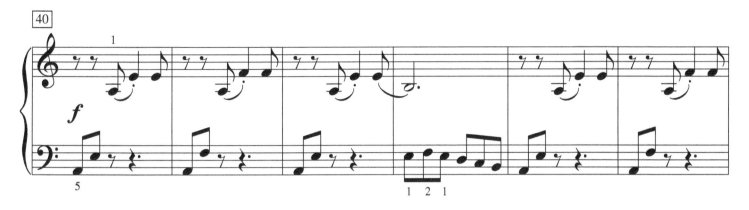

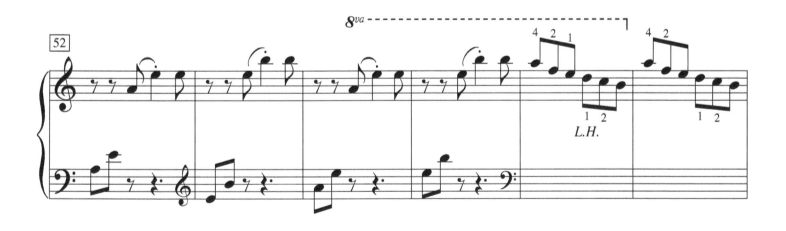

The Icy Rings of Saturn

Carolyn Miller

Eerily, at a moderate tempo

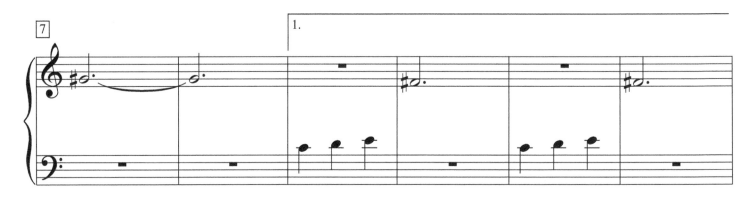

hold pedal down continuously

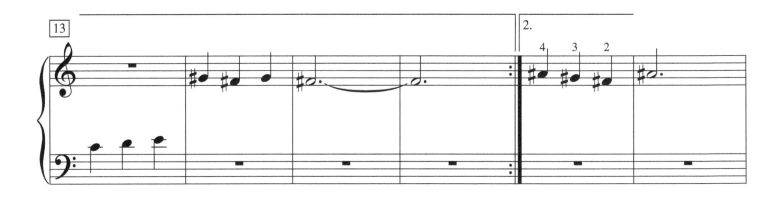

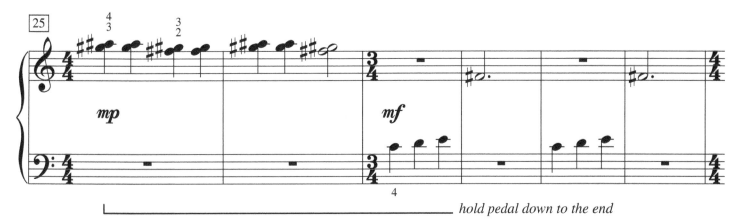

hold pedal down to the end

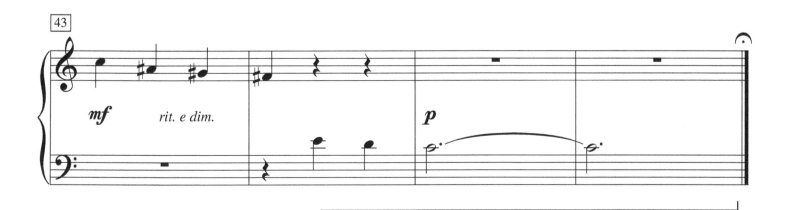

Uranus Spinning

Carolyn Miller

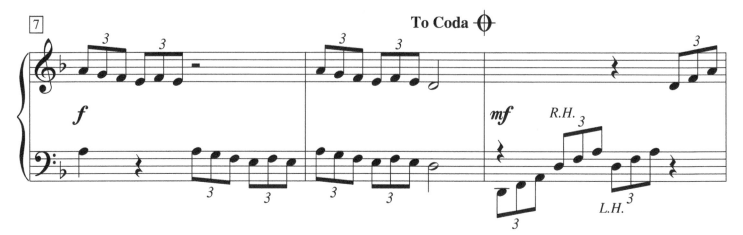

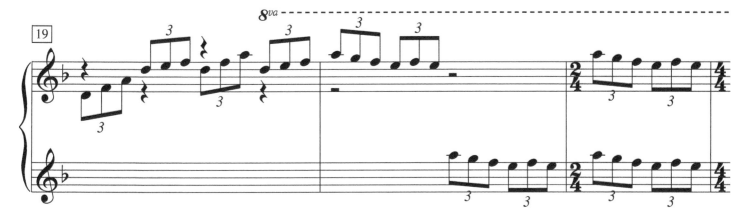

The Winds of Neptune

Carolyn Miller

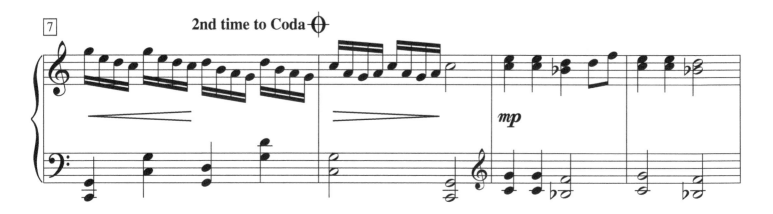

23

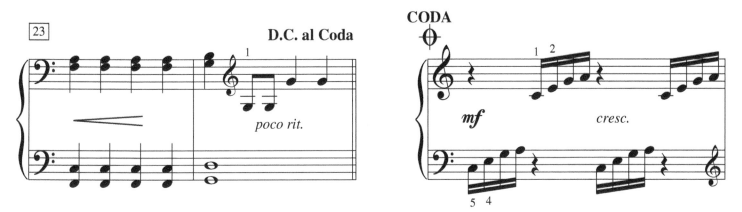

CAROLYN MILLER'S teaching and composing career spans over 40 prolific years. She holds music degrees from both the College Conservatory of Music at the University of Cincinnati and Xavier University. Carolyn regularly presents workshops throughout the United States and is a frequent adjudicator at festivals and competitions. Although she recently retired from the Ohio public school system, she continues to maintain her own private studio.

Carolyn's music emphasizes fundamental technical skills for advancing pianists, young and old, and is remarkably fun to play. This may explain why well-known television personality Regis Philbin studied and performed her pieces on national television in the early 1990s. Carolyn's compositions continue to appear frequently on state contest lists, as well as on the popular NFMC Festivals Bulletin. She is listed in the *Who's Who in America* and *Who's Who of American Women*.